THE
BRAND AMBASSADOR
HANDBOOOK

By Edwin J. Goitia

Acknowledgements

First and foremost I want to thank my fiancée and the kids for putting up with my crazy schedule, erratic travel itineraries, and the fast-pace of my world and my work for the past 5 years since I have been with you guys. It has been an incredible journey and you have only made me that much stronger and wiser. Through many phone calls and Facetime chats, we all stayed close and I appreciate your support. I love you all very dearly.

Long drives, crazy adventures, and many, many tents later, I would be amiss to forget to recognize those who have helped me along the way in my journey. After many long days and nights, beer flights at random bars and restaurants across the country, and meeting thousands of people, I couldn't have done it without a select few.

To my buddy Anthony Gomez, who taught me that what we do is "the closest thing to being a rockstar". His passion for creativity, helping others and travel has surpassed anything that I could ever imagine out a friend within the promotional marketing space. Co-Founder of SODO Marketing, Anthony continues to represent what is great within our industry, and the possibilities with travel hacking, tour management, and being a power couple with his lovely wife, Adrienne. Thank you Anthony and Adrienne!

Happiness can be achieved as a brand ambassador and event manager, as has been shown by my good friend Pete Sengoba. Pete has always been there for me, and continues to have a huge smile and an incredible sense of humor. My buddy Pete is a constant reminder that even with hard work and dedication, and simultaneously enjoying a vibrant and fulfilling life, it is possible to be extremely happy in one's endeavors AND still live the life you want.

To Sherman Fantroy, for guiding me in pursuit of my higher passions and for pushing my limits to the next level. You truly taught me that to strive for perfection is only a small, yet vital part, to every event activation and marketing campaign. To truly create an unforgettable experience that will reverberate across the masses and impress the many is what we were born to do, as you have taught me. Philosophy, passion, and perfection are just some of the things you have shown me the way towards. Our friendship is of the highest value to me and I look forward to doing great things together for years to come.

Finally, thanks to the thousands of other event marketers, brand ambassadors, tour managers, account managers, and marketing directors who have blessed me with their presence and shared their perspectives, the amazing stories, and contributed incredible experiences. To name a few: Nisha Sanjuro, for sharing your kindness and teaching me patience; Chris & Dayana Perry, for showing me the way of Miami; Daniel Matson, for your youthful drive and entrepreneurial spirit; Daniel Philips, for innovation in the endurance event space; Robert J Adams, for leading the way in Vegas and being a fellow compadre in entrepreneurial pursuits and seeing the bigger picture; Patrick Hesse for the great laughs and paving the path in comedy and events; Angelique Deleon, for being a loyal foot-soldier in the field and for believing & sharing the Promo Rockstar vision with thousands of others whenever you get the opportunity; Heather Diesel, for being a part of the bigger vision and striving for greatness in your own way; Jermaine Hampton, for being an early adopter to the Promo Rockstar way and putting your professional development to the test, with great results in the end; and finally, Emily Bendus, for believing that anything was possible and going from a no one in promotional marketing to someone valuable and picking up tons of gigs in just your first 3 months from inception.

Of course, thank you to our readers, for contributing your time, energy, and enthusiasm to learning the Promo Rockstar way and for sharing our vision with others, in hopefully helping contribute to their success, in as much as your very own moving forward. Together, we all succeed and live a life only most would dream of.

Table of Contents

Preface

The Grand Deception

My Story

Introduction

PART I: Foundation

Basics of Brand Ambassadorship

Full Time/Part Time

Payment Structure

The Golden Rules

Ethics and Responsibilities

The Privileges

Inside Your Closet

The Promo Rockstar Lifestyle

Tips and Tricks

PART II: Next-Level Brand Ambassadorship

Start a Revolution

What Does It Take?

Can You Do It?

Time To Grab Your Bootstraps

PART III: Questionnaire & Notes

To my mother and father…
who taught me the value of taking care of the people we meet in our lives. And that with hard work, grit, and enormous energy, anything is possible.

Preface

When was the last time that you got paid for telling your friends about the latest iPhone that was out? Or that cool new Coach purse? What if I told you you've been living a lie your entire life? The truth is: you *can* get paid for word-of-mouth marketing. The question is, how? This Brand Ambassador Handbook will show you the way.

This is the story of what it takes to be a superstar as what is not as commonly known, "a brand ambassador". The know-how and tips and tricks in what it takes to take it to the next level in the world of experiential marketing. What exactly is experiential marketing? That, my friend, is the perfect question.

Experiential marketing is a world where not many venture, a world where you can take a simple idea and be able to show it to the world. Not just any idea, however. A hot idea that, along with a smile and a handshake, can change the lives of many for years to come. The experience is amazing (ex. experiential). No one would ever think that such a short transaction in time and energy between two people could be so profound. Talking to an individual about the latest craze, the hottest trend, or a must-have product out in the market may not seem like the most fun thing to do. Yet, we've been doing it every single day...ever since we were born! How would you feel if I told you that you've been a part of the world's largest scheme? (More on that in a bit)

Funny enough, there are times where I can approach an individual about the latest laptop or cell phone and tell them all about it. 70 out of 100 people will take a moment to smile and listen to me. 20 out of 100 will actually give me about 10 seconds of their time. 9 out of 100 will actually take the time to have a conversation about the product and walk away having a much better perception of the brand. 1 out of 100 people will tell me "I don't believe you, it's all a scheme." I laugh when I hear these words, smile, and tell the person to have a great day. If they only knew...

The Grand Deception

There are 6 Billion people on this amazing planet we call Earth. Then, you have 500 companies that rake in billions of dollars a year and the majority of that money is held captive by a select few upper-hierarchy executive members of said companies. Meanwhile, millions of people out there in society are working for these companies…and they don't even know it.

YOU have been selling products since you were a child. Hell, since you were born. Your parents would dress you up in the latest baby clothing line called Baby Rump (not a real company, we checked), a pair of Air Jack shoes, and even let you ride in style in the hottest baby stroller in the marketplace. They take you out for a walk to the park, and as they are walking, their neighbors and friends walk by and say hi. They would stop by and see how cute you looked. In fact, they thought you were so cute, that you immediately made a brand impression on them (subconsciously speaking, that is). Now, they are head over heels for baby-sized Air Jack's, the new Baby Rump clothing line (they just have to have it!), and they absolutely want that cool stroller when they have a baby. Perhaps this said couple that saw you and were bedazzled by your baby-wear and your sweet baby ride are now planning on having kids soon and even have a baby registry online. They go home, with the image of the cool products they saw still stamped freshly in their mind, and immediately login to their registry and add these products. Boom! You made your first sale, AS A BABY, without even trying. Now, where is your commission for that sale? Oh wait, you didn't get one? "That's just crazy, I didn't sell anything", you tell yourself. I beg to differ. Every single person on this planet has been conditioned to sell since they were practically a zygote.

Now think of all the things that you have "sold" for these big companies since you were a little kid. That cool iPod you had? You probably sold dozens of those just by carrying it around. Oh, and that sweet new Lidso hats you were donning during your teenage years at parties? Maybe sold a hundred of those. If you were paid for every brand impression you provided for these companies over the years, you would be rich. Unfortunately, it doesn't work that way.

However, there is something you can do about it.

*Fictional company names used for example purposes.

My Story

Hi, my name is Edwin J. Goitia, founder of Promo Rockstars (formerly known as Super Promotional Rockstars! 2010). Back in 2006, I graduated from Batavia High School with two scholarships to my #2 college choice, Augustana College (I had lost a tie for a full-ride scholarship to the University of Chicago, an ivy-league school, and my #1 choice). I was just a normal guy with big dreams and aspirations. I grew up working hard in school, even working two jobs in high school, while involved in sports and music the the same time.

When I got to Augustana, I tried taking more courses than most people, was involved in half a dozen campus organizations, and was even a frat boy. I was so involved that I got ambitious and even tried starting my own business while attending school full-time. All of my friends thought I was crazy and event tried talking me out of it. I was so driven and had such crazy tunnel vision, that I proceeded to try and grow the business full-time on top of my studies. It even got to the point where I started neglecting school a bit. I was traveling everywhere, taking huge risks, and eventually going $20,000 into debt. At the end of my first year of college, I had no idea how I was going to afford school the following year. I tried working things out with the school, attempted to get more scholarships, all to no avail.

I ended up taking a year off school to try and grow my network marketing business and went into even more debt. From 2007-2008, I dabbled with promotional marketing here and there, but did not think I could make it into a full-time deal. I found myself working at a Krispy Kremes full-time to make ends meet, eventually registering at a community college and took some more courses. I quickly got bored, however, and went back and forth with community college, dropping it altogether. School just wasn't that exciting for me.

Eventually, I worked extremely hard at Krispy Kreme, moving up to an assistant manager and even being promised a position as General Manager. Abruptly, I got laid off from the restaurant job in 2008, after being promised a promotion with higher pay. I was left with nothing. I was struggling so badly, I would do anything for money. I did door-to-door sales for a telecommunication company full time for over a year for several companies, working for commissions and also working part-time desk jobs and any gigs I could get my hand on. This was a rough time in my life.

Then, one day, something happened. I had been spending so much time honing my mindset and training myself to think more like an entrepreneur, reading books by the dozens, spending my free time perfecting my skills, and listening to successful coaches, that I had a complete breakthrough. I got focused, dropped everything, and even when it seemed that I could not do promotional work full-time for the life of me, I decided I was going to do whatever it took to make it happen. And so I did.

Fast-forward 5 years later, everything that I had dreamed, everything that I had envisioned, had become true. I've personally completed 4 national tours, 2 regional tours, been a brand ambassador, an emcee, a costume character, a sign-spinner, a street performer, a musician, a surveyor, a presenter, a tech specialist, you name it. What a journey it has been.

Why am I telling you all of this?

For the reason that I want everyone to know that I am not perfect. I am a human being just like everyone else. I've failed. I've been down in the dumps. I've almost quit many, many times. I almost quit doing promotions completely back in 2009. I know what struggle feels like, and let me tell you, it sucks. Knowing how badly it sucks, I promised myself back in 2010, once I became full time early in the year, that I would do everything to give back to the industry and to make a huge impact in the lives of many. I knew that if I just gave back enough, I would make thousand's of people's lives at least somewhat easier. I would teach others to avoid the same costly mistakes I made. I promised myself that I would spend as much time as possible helping others more than I helped myself. It was a gift, and I had to share it with the world. Then, it became my life's mission. It became everything I wanted to be.

Introduction

Thank you for taking the time to read my story. It was not easy to tell it while I sat down and poured my heart and soul into it. Like anything else, though, it's gratifying to share it knowing how far I've come. Also, it's even more amazing to know how many of my closest compadres in the field I have impacted and how many friends I have helped from struggling to making near six-figures a year or more.

The Brand Ambassador Handbook is a compilation of the philosophies and some practical knowledge that I like to teach those that cross my path in the field. At least, those who were curious enough to ask and learn. Please keep this somewhere where you can refer to when times get tough. Perhaps you could use a different perception or something to help guide you when you get stuck mentally, emotionally, or career-wise.

All while we teach you how you can take full advantage of learning how to be the best brand ambassador you can be. Keep in mind: although the term "brand ambassador" is used generically throughout the handbook, this book can apply to you if you are a model, DJ, bartender, emcee, dancer, singer, radio announcer, consultant, or any other type of creative individual.

With that said, I hope that the Brand Ambassador Handbook can be of some value to you on your journey. Good luck and good activating!

PART I
Foundation

Basics of Brand Ambassadorship

Being a brand ambassador is like being an entrepreneur, and partly a freelancer. You are essentially in business for yourself, to an extent. There is virtually no overhead, and realistically the only money you invest in your venture is in professional training (only if required for a role, like acting classes, etc.), a gym membership, clothing, perhaps transportation (such as a car), gas, a laptop, and a cell phone. Those are the bare minimums.

As a brand ambassador, you are essentially a brand evangelist hired out by a talent agency and given the task of going out into the public (usually during a live, planned event, and at times, in a guerilla marketing scenario) and spreading the message of a brand or service.

It's as simple as showing up early, being clean-cut and presentable with a smile, following the directions of the program (learning the branding message, etc.), engaging the most that you can (while being energetic), and positively conveying the brand messaging to consumers around you. Of course, none of this would be as enjoyable if you weren't having fun at the same time.

Now, if you are new to this, you are probably wondering, "Ok, that is great! But what are the events like? What exactly will I be doing?" That's a great question and the answer is that "No two events are ever the same." Therefore, you will be working in a fast-paced, highly flexible environment where anything can happen and changes sometimes occur last minute. However, it is all fun and people have a great time! You will be a part of making sure that events are high-energy and full of great people such as yourself.

Full Time or Part Time?

Another common question is "Is this a full-time deal or only part-time? How does it work?" The answer is that it's completely up to you. You basically structure your schedule (for the most part) and are accountable for filling your calendar. This is not a regular 9-to-5 and you will not get paid every 2 weeks (in most cases, some long-term programs do pay weekly/bi-weekly).

Essentially, if you know you want to take a one-month vacation this year, you just work hard in the meantime and then structure your schedule to accommodate your travel desires, time with family, or whatever it may be. You call the shots. Now, if you are on a long-term program, most likely you agreed to be available for the full-extent of that time, and so you must adhere to that. From time to time, you may work with a company that is flexible in that area, if you want to take some time off.

The benefit of working part-time is that you can work another full-time job and, on your free time (evenings/weekends, for example) you can pick up some part-time gigs to make extra money.
The benefit of going full-time is that you can work a part-time gig on the side or even go to school at the same time. Also, you will sometimes be eligible for perks or bonuses when you work long-term full-time programs. Also, some gigs compensate for travel/mileage, and that can help alleviate work expenses, as well.

Either way, the flexibility in our industry is very much like being a freelancer and is a great lifestyle to look forward to.

Payment Structure

As mentioned before, the payment structure and scheduling in the promotional marketing industry varies and can take some organization.

Essentially, the average pay period can range from 2 weeks to 8 weeks maximum. Luckily, more and more companies are lessening the amount of time it takes to pay their talent, and 2-4 weeks is becoming the popular pay period. Of course, there are still companies that take longer than a month, even two months to pay.

Why so long for payment, you ask? Usually, you will be dealing with the middle man (staffing agency) and so they do not directly deal with the budget for a program to pay their staff. Essentially, you (the talent) works the event, and then send in timesheets (or an invoice) to the staffing agency. The agency then takes all of the timesheets and consolidates it into one big invoice to send to the marketing firm (or the client, in some cases) and must wait 2-4 weeks for a payment to be issued. Then there is another 1-2 week turnaround time as the agency lets the check clear and in turn, issues checks to their talent (which is YOU!).

Another method of payment that speeds things up is direct deposit. This is also becoming a popular option across companies, and in some cases, Paypal is even an option. One of the lesser known but also possible options, is to receive a branded debit-card with a company and get paid directly on the card.

The Golden Rules

Every industry should have a list of commandments, or golden rules.

Here's our take on the Golden Rules for promotional marketing:

- Thou shall think in terms of abundance when looking for gigs.
- Thou shall pass on gigs not working to others in need.
- Thou shall deliver their best work possible at all times.
- Thou shall maintain a positive integrity and relationship with talent and staffing agencies for years to come.
- Thou will not be unethical during promotional events.

- Thou will fill out all paperwork prior to, during, and after activation to the best of your ability.
- Thou will always take photos before/during/after an event for records and also for the company.
- Thou will always engage in every way possible and not be lazy during an event.
- Thou will take care of event assets and elements as best as possible.
- Thou will follow up with companies and pick up phone calls at all times.
- Thou shall show up to activations early, and not just on time.
- Thou will be respectful to staffing agencies, client, and talent staff.
- Thou will be professional at events, yet have fun at the same time.
- Thou will not abuse managerial responsibilities/perks.
- Thou shall deliver on promises made.
- Thou shall not disappear during breaks at events. Make sure that your manager can find you.
- Thou shall not call in last minute to cancel an event, unless a true last-minute emergency.
- Thou shall only accept offers to work an event if they are truly committed to work (not knowing you will have to quit in between the program due to a vacation or another program).
- Thou shalt be as presentable and clean-cut as possible when working promotional gigs.
- Thou shall not be caught at an event with arms crossed and disengaging with the consumer audience.
- Thou shall present self in the most honest way possible on their resume/cover letter.

Ethics and Responsibilities

In promotional marketing (especially for new peeps), it can be mind-blowing the responsibilities that we are given, and especially the assets and elements of an event that we are entrusted to.

Ipads, cameras, and dongles, oh my! It's easy to get excited over all of it and even forget to be careful with the equipment you're given to use during an event. You must always remember to treat everything with care and as if it were your very own. Companies spend thousands of dollars on all the elements that make up an entire event, so the least you can do is show them respect by taking care of their equipment.

iPads should always have a cover (although, sometimes, the company does not provide one). If they don't, you have to take extra caution where you place it or how you hold it. You never want to just walk away from any expensive electronics or premiums that are part of an event. As much as we hate to admit it, consumers sometimes steal these assets. The more precautions you take now, the least likely it is to happen.

This can apply to premiums (also called freemiums) such as vouchers, gift cards, prizes, t-shirts, you name it. Not only do you have to be responsible, you must take care that none of the team members violate their responsibilities or rights and take premiums or expensive electronic assets with them. Even if you are just a brand ambassador, reporting theft to the manager can save a whole program from falling apart. The issue would be addressed right away, and everybody can go about his or her days happily and without too much chaos.

If you are dealing with laptops/tablets, ensure that they are locked down somehow or at the very least, attended to. Walking away from laptops and televisions can be a bad idea, especially around large crowds. Even when devices are locked down, you would be surprised how many unattended locked devices are stolen every year. It is best to have at least 1 person attending these devices at all times.

Also, if you know an event will be closing soon and there will be no overnight security, make sure that management takes the devices with them or that someone is protecting the devices.

It is unfortunate that things like this happen, but the best thing we can do is to prevent it from happening in the first place. By being organized, on point, and attentive to your surroundings, you should be able to enjoy your events without worrying about stolen or misplaced goods.

The Privileges

Sometimes, the privileges that we are allowed in the field can shock newcomers. Half hour to hour-long breaks? What the heck? Free entry into an event? Sure! The chance to participate in other cool perks? Heck yea! All of these can make our jobs seem like a dream fantasy and all of a sudden, the work mentality goes out the window. Make sure this doesn't happen to you.

Although everything seems fun and like a vacation, you still have to be professional and show up early to work, as well as work hard during the event. If you are brand new to this industry, it is very easy to get caught up in the alternative lifestyle, want to shoot selfies all the time, get caught up with engaging with consumers, and so on and so forth. As long as you remember that you are there to accomplish a goal and deliver for a client, all will be well.

Inside Your Closet

There are a few items you may want to stock your closet with as you prepare to get started with promotions. If you plan to work primarily as a brand ambassador, these are some things you'll definitely want to have handy:

- Khaki pants and shorts (not cargo, unless stated acceptable)
- Black dress slacks
- Solid black/white sneakers, with little or no branding
- Black/white long sleeve shirt for layering in the cold
- White dress shirt, if you plan to work higher scale events
- Plain blue jeans (not distressed denim or with any holes)

These items can be used over and over again, making it worth the investment (which likely won't be much, anyway!). It's very important to show up in proper uniform. "I don't have that," is not an acceptable excuse for such a simple wardrobe, so head to the store if you need to pick up some new khakis or sneakers. Better to always keep the client happy! Nobody wants to be sent home or have his or her check dinged.

While most events will provide their staff with branded apparel to wear, you will typically only receive a brand T-shirt unless otherwise specified. Wear something that will be comfortable under a T-shirt, like a tank top or a thin shirt, in the event that there is no accessible place to change out of whatever you are already wearing. If it's chilly out, layer up so you can shed as needed for the weather and temperature conditions.

Of course, we also have to talk about our infamous khakis, right? Khaki pants/shorts tend to be the standard for this industry, therefore it's ideal to have at least a couple pairs. (Sure, they aren't always sexy, but we know you can rock them!) Guys: don't wear cargo pants unless the agency says in their event description that this is okay. Ladies: all shorts should be a conservative length. Make sure whatever you buy is comfortable, because you're likely to be wearing them a lot. You should also have a pair of nice, casual blue jeans if your agency prefers those instead. Stay away from the distressed appearance or anything with holes. Basic is always better when you're going for a professional look.

Before leaving your promo at the end of the day, don't forget to ask your manager if you're able to take the branded gear home with you. Usually, if it's just a T-Shirt, the agency won't ask for the shirt back but it won't hurt to check. If you are wearing a hoodie or something a bit more expensive, always confirm before you clock out, as it may be deducted from your paycheck if you take apparel home that you were supposed to return. It will also inconvenience the agency and cost more money if they only have a delegated amount for gear and that gear begins to disappear. If you want to get more promo jobs, always show up ready to work in uniform, and be sure to return all borrowed clothing.

The Rockstar Lifestyle

Imagine yourself waking up everyday, wondering what your day is going to bring. I mean, literally. What the heck are you going to do today? You don't have to worry about going to a boring 9-to-5, hoping that things aren't the same as yesterday, scared that you will be bored out of your wits having to be a mechanical robot and quite frankly just not even enjoying life anymore? Sounds fun doesn't it?

Unfortunately, this is the reality for many people out there. They live life Monday through Friday just like this, hoping that things will be better next week. They expunge themselves in liquor, family events, nightlife, and sometimes chaos in order to forget what happened during there past week on the job. Then Sunday night comes, and all fear, doubt and uncertainty clouds the mind of the unfortunate victim, creating an unwanted mindset of not ever wanting to go back to work again. Yet, people do it anyways. Why?

Why do average people go back to work knowing that it not what they desire? Why do many settle and just do the seemingly inevitable and go back to the "cubicle lifestyle", knowing that nothing is going to change?

Is it because of bills and debt that has been accumulated, no doubt to college education, new cars and maybe a new home? Or is it because we grow up hearing from our parents that the right way to live life is to just accept the status quo and go to school, get good grades, and get a good...job.

Really? "It can't be!," I thought to myself over and over again after leaving college near the end of my freshman year. I was a college dropout. I had took on some business ventures in the hopes that there was light at the end of the tunnel. It caused me inner emotional pain at first to see that I was taking the less attractive route of leaving school. Maybe I would be the next Steve Jobs? Who knew? The only thing that I knew was that I was in for the ride of my life.

Most college students and graduates dream of finishing school and traveling the world, seeing all the things that maybe their parents may not have had the pleasure of doing. Parents and baby boomers alike oftentimes encourage these students to see the world and experience all they can before "life" happens to them. Some listen, many don't.

Recently, a good friend of mine from high school had hit me up on Facebook and was curious as to how I got to travel so much, see the world, and be happy while doing it all. "How do you do it? What the heck is it that you really do?", he asked me. If I had a dime for every time that someone asked me that question, I would be rich. People ask me this question every...single...day. That is when I decided that it was time to create a resource that I could point to when people *really* wanted to understand what it was that I truly did. To learn about the lifestyle of the promotional marketer.

Ah, the lifestyle. Back in 2012, my good friend Anthony Gomez and I were having a deep discussion about what the industry had done for us and how much it had changed our lives. The things that we were able to see, the people we had the pleasure of meeting, the friends we were blessed to have made along the path. He then told me something I would never forget. "What we do is the closest thing to being a rockstar." My eyes literally opened and my heart skipped a beat. "Wow, I never thought of it that way," I replied to him in earnest.

Living life like a rockstar? What?! I thought this book was about how to get into event marketing', you are probably thinking to yourself right about. Don't worry. I am not going to veer too far off track. Give me a chance to explain myself here. When you imagine a rockstar lifestyle, what do you think about? Most people would imagine the unlimited traveling, the free swag, the raving fans, countless friends, getting VIP access to the top venues around, and everything that encompasses celebrity status and fame. I thought of all of this, and then it hit me right in the face. We were rockstars, alright. Maybe we weren't famous or celebrities. However, we were definitely rockstars for all the brands we represented.

When you see a Doritos* commercial, for example, have you seen an actor (usually male) taking a Doritos chip out of a bag and looking at it, literally drooling over the cheesy tortilla chip, staring at it in insurmountable disbelief, wondering what amazing experience awaited him? Then he takes a huge bite, putting the entire Doritos in his mouth, whereas the audience hears a loud "crunch!" and everyone who watches the commercial is experience the same sensations at the exact same time in, most likely, the same measure as the actor.

The person sitting at home can literally *taste, feel, and touch* that Doritos thanks to the *experience*. The experience is everything when it comes to sharing a branding message. That one man in the commercial who takes the dramatic bite of the fantastically ever-lasting Doritos chip literally created an *experience* for millions of television-viewers from the comfort of their living room couch. What do you think that person does next time they are at the store and see the chip aisle? They go straight for the Doritos of course! (In extreme cases, they would immediately jump in their car and head to the closest convenience store for a bag of Doritos following the commercial).

What's the point I am trying to get across? Good question. The point I am trying to make here is that *anyone* can be a rockstar. Yes, even *you*. "Me? No way!" Yes, *you*. You, my friend, *are* a rockstar. Think about it. From the moment you were born, you essentially became what we like to call a *promotional model*. Your parents dressed you up in the latest styles, perhaps bought you the latest crib, stroller, toys, a super-absorbent diaper, the coolest little baby gloves that kept you from scratching your face, amazing Mozart music to put you to sleep (perhaps built into the crib itself?), even the newest baby Air Jordan's, and the list goes on and on and on. It's mind-boggling actually.

Young parents are without a doubt the best product evangelists out there in society today. Your parents were most likely going around telling *everybody* about all the things they were buying for you, and how cute you looked, and how adorable this toy is, and how stylish this and that is on you, etc., etc., etc.

All those years, your parents were soft selling other parents and especially soon-to-be parents, on all these wonderful products that were in the marketplace (out of thousands of possible choices!). Surely enough, your parents friends, coworkers, family members and their direct circle of influence were highly trusting of their opinions and so they did some of their own product research.

They wanted to see what all the buzz was about. They needed to go ahead and validate all of this so they went to the store, or searched online, or asked their friends or family members. Any way that they could get confirmation of what they heard to get them even sold. Guess what? You were practically a model as a baby. Your parents friends and family members were so excited about seeing you and what you looked like and all the cool stuff that you had, that they just *had* to go see you for themselves. As soon as they saw the super-elastic expandable diaper that could hold a gallon of baby fluids (not really) and your baby Air Jordan's that could allow you to crawl at the speed of Jordan (ok, maybe), they were instantly sold.

Their hearts were won, perhaps they were in tears because you were just so darned cute, and their check cards and credit cards were practically already in hand. You were a baby rockstar and literally just made multi-million dollar companies a sale. Congratulations!

But you see, the journey did not end there. Oh no. The trends kept on rockin' and rollin' and you most likely just kept on keeping up with them. Now, there are a great number of people out there who claim they do not keep up with fashion trends and tech trends and whatnot.

However, I always note that no matter how uninvolved you may actually be in the purchasing of a trendy product or service, you are surely *talking* about it. When leaving feedback (positive *and* negative), or talking to friends, or even checking it out online, you are essentially feeding energy to the hype, in some way or another.

That's how powerful brand messaging is. No matter how a product is portrayed by consumers, it will always grab attention through the use of video and pictures alone....

Tips and Tricks

- Make sure to always portray your best self-image possible in your resume, in a professional manner.

- Ensure to engage in social media and company websites as much as possible.

- Network at all times. You never know whom you will run into.

- Have business cards on you at all times. People will take you more seriously.

- Always bring extra khaki pants or black casual/dress pants with you. You never know when you might get a last minute event-booking request.

- Carry copies of your resume with you or on your smartphone to be able to share at a moments notice. (Even better, always have a pre-filled I9 or W2 to send out at a moments notice.)

- Download mobile apps to make life easier (such as Catch, SignNow, and Genius Scan)

- Always have an emergency bag packed for those last-minute travelling gigs.

- Make sure your car's maintenance is up-to-date before getting on long term programs (oil change, tire pressure checked, full tank of gas, money saved for gas expenses)

- Carry sunscreen for hot-climate outdoor events and Heat Packs for winter events in cold-climate areas.

- It's a good idea to carry a pocket knife/box cutter, a screwdriver, zip ties, tape, permanent marker and maybe even a hammer/mallet in your car. These tools, although you might not use them much, can save an activation from time to time. (Bonus for carrying bottles of water with you).
- Always bring your phone charger with you and/or backup charging cases or battery packs. (This could be essential not just for smartphones, but tablets and laptops too).

PART II
Next-Level Brand Ambassadorship

Start A Revolution

So you think the economy sucks. Boo-hoo. So does everyone else.

That's old news.

What are you going to do about it?

Are you just going to sit there and cry in agony and pain? Or are you going to bolster up the courage and make something happen?

Most people would rather live their lives going to their 9-5s and coming home, sitting on the couch, watching TV, and doing it all over again. Not the event marketer.

Whether you are unemployed, underemployed, overemployed, self-employed, a freelancer, a contractor, or just plain looking for an active lifestyle, event marketing might just be the answer.

Ask yourself these key questions:

Do I like to have fun?
Do I like entertainment?
Do I like free stuff?
Do I like to travel?
Do I like traveling for free or close to it?
Do I like getting VIP access to the nation's biggest events?
Do I like meeting new people?
Do I like to sport a smile?
Can I engage with people in an excited way in different environments?

If you answered "yes" to all of these questions, then you may just be a fit for the event industry. However, there's so much more that we will be covering in this compendium of event marketing knowledge.

Anywho, back to the subject. I'm a 26-year-old self-employed event marketer, enjoy listening to classical music while drinking beer and wine, and am an avid runner, even enjoying the occasional run outside in the snowy streets of Chicago during the winters.

I enjoy my cup of coffee every single morning, staring out the window wondering what possibilities the day will bring. My usual morning routine, even when hectic and busy, is to read my horoscopes, some motivational quotes, and connect with new people online and introduce myself.
I enjoy the occasional debate on the Renaissance, quantum physics, and the annexation of Puerto Rico.

As you can see, I'm just a regular guy with big dreams and aspirations. To help people like yourself really dive into the possibilities that event marketing has to offer. This book is merely to introduce you to the lifestyle that you can have.

So you are here because you are looking for change. You are looking for something to hold on to with dear life that will change the outlook you have on everything in life.

You, my friend, are looking for a REVOLUTION.

Yes, a revolution.

Your life is either bland or you are looking for an adventure. Maybe your love life isn't going that great or maybe your significant other and you just need some time apart to discover yourselves.

Perhaps you're in college or contemplating on going back to grad school and you want to be able to supplement your income without having to kill yourself with a full-time job or two part-time jobs, as I have seen many do over the years.

Why should you have to take another job that you will most likely hate even doing and then having to quit?

Or maybe you're stuck at your current job making minimum wage, wondering if there is another way of life that should be lived. Trust me, I was there.

Whatever it is, you need to be thrown for a complete loop in your life. It would be as if you were to do a complete 360 and start a new life.

Enter event marketing, otherwise known as "promotional modeling", "promotional marketing", "street marketing", "guerilla marketing", "tradeshow modeling", and much much more.

The world of event marketing is an exciting one, and very fulfilling at that. There is so much that can be learned, so many skills that can be honed, so many talents that can be developed, and the opportunities that present themselves are perfect for those who are looking for more excitement and more stories to create in their lifetime.

Many have asked myself, usually on a daily basis, exactly what it is that I do and how it is that I can get to travel so much. I am sure this is the case for so many event marketers out there. The envy from our closest friends and family, sometimes from people we have not spoken for years, is enough to reflect on our lifestyles and how blessed we really are.

Many college students dream about graduating from school and being able to take off into the world, traveling the U.S. and eventually the world. Heck, I never thought about it, but one can travel the world all while creating an income and enjoying every minute of it, as well. Did I look at it that way when I was in school? Not really. Most people don't. Usually, the preparations go something like this:

Scenario A: Save and go
Work hard for a couple of years working a mediocre job.
Save up some money and live below your means.
When you have saved enough to travel around the world for 6 months to a year, sell most or all of one's personal belongings (or put it into storage), maybe put a bit of money aside as an emergency fund, and then take off and backpack through Europe or go on an All-American tour.

Scenario B: Study Abroad
During the last two years of college, start applying for overseas English exchange programs.
Consider and weigh all options in terms of which country (or countries) to visit.
Take out a loan or get a special student loan (specifically geared towards study abroad programs).
Enjoy the travels, meet new people and maybe learn a new language.

Scenario C: Event Marketing
Work locally or anywhere you like (your choice)
Make amazing money
Pay off student loans and become debt-free
Travel the U.S. and the world and see everything you've ever wanted to see while still making money.
Have amazing experiences while learning how to do it cheap/free.

After seeing the above scenarios, which seems most appealing to you? I know, I know. You're most likely wondering "What the heck is event marketing?"

Before we dive head-deep into this wonderful world, let's quickly look first at the above scenarios:

With Options A and B, things take time and they consist of waiting to either make money to be able to afford the travels or to take out a loan or finance your travels in some way, which require paying them back in the future.
Also, with the first two options, you are looking at much uncertainty, many unforeseen expenses, and sometimes, the experiences and options become

limited with the entry-level type income most college graduates experience in the beginning right after departing college.

With Option C, you can start traveling while you make money ASAP. Not many other options out there will give you that chance. Along with that, there are an infinite number of possibilities out there in terms of geographic location, experiences that can be nearly customized and/or laser-targeted to your tastes, preferences and skills and/or talents.

So, let me ask you again: Which sounds more appealing?

Option A? If this is your answer, then I wish you much luck in your endeavors. While you take 6 months to a year or longer (I've seen many friends save up for almost 2 years or more before they decide to finally jump and take a trip, no matter how much of a dent it would take on their finances or how much uncertainty there was as to how bills would be paid or how savings would be affected in the decision to travel).

Option B? Seems like the next best option right? When I was in my freshman year of college I thought this was a dream. While taking Japanese foreign classes and learning the language inside and out, I found out I had the opportunity to travel abroad in Asia , visiting six continents and engulfing myself in their culture. Amazing, right? That's what I thought.

I tried so hard to figure out how I could possibly afford a 6-month trip around Asia that cost several thousand dollars. I had no idea how I was even going to be able to afford my sophomore year of college! I was determined to make the trip happen however, to no avail, and was saddened when I fell short of the trip cost by several hundred dollars.

I beat myself up, thinking that I should have taken out a loan to fund the trip. Thank god that I did not go that route. Many of my friends took out loans (or had their parents do so, in most cases), blew all of their financial aid money, or asked their family to help them get the money. I'm more than certain that some of these folks are still paying for these loans, 3 years after graduating, for a trip that was taken back in 2007 during their freshman/sophomore year.

My point? What's the point of taking one awesome trip and paying it back for years to come? Why not taking lots of smaller trips and pay as you go? Just my opinion.

Option C: Go crazy, work anywhere, and make great money. Back in 2007, I first got into the promotional marketing game. I was unsure if it was a scam, or for real, or what it was. All I know was that I was going to make something of it. I got offered my first gig with Nescafe Dolce Gusto. I thought it was exciting, my adrenaline pumping at the thought of trying something so unique, so new. It was unlike any job I had ever taken on. Fast forward to 2009. Two years have passed by, I've been working the promo gigs on and off, with a full-time restaurant management job as my primary income. I wasn't feeling like I was going to make it. Maybe promotional work was just not for me, I thought to myself. Maybe I just wasn't cut out for it. Maybe I should pursue a different career path.

What Does It Take?

So, one of the biggest misconceptions in this industry when a newbie runs into it, and realizes how much fun it can be and it how it would solve all their problems is that everything is easy, carefree and can be done by anyone. The biggest letdown is when they find out how much work truly goes into staying busy and networking.

The one thing I will say right here and now is that the event marketing industry is not for everyone. Some people are made for it, others are not. You will never know, until you try. Just like anything new, you must be willing to try it out and really give it everything you have. When stepping out of your comfort zone, I can assure you there is always a bit of fear, anxiety and discomfort with anything that is new and unfamiliar territory. By expanding your horizons and really being open-minded of the possibilities, you can open doors to opportunities you never thought possible. Flexibility in thinking is definitely key if you are to get to that point.

So, what does this all mean you ask?

Well, first of all, this is a legitimate industry with a legitimate business opportunity. Now, I like to use the term "business opportunity" not in the sense of an MLM opportunity, but rather in the sense that you will essentially own your own business. Let's take a step back for a second, if the sound of "owning your own business" nearly makes you want to faint. I'm not talking about you having to own a brick and mortar business, and hire employees, and all of that. The opportunity can be there years down the road, but that's not what we are talking about right now.

Most people in today's society forget that we are all salespeople and we all have a brand that we represent. What brand is that, you ask? Well, the brand of ME of course! Every day that you wake up and go to school, or go to work, or even go volunteer at a local shelter, you are instilling your brand into everything you do, and with everyone that you run across. If your name is Billy Bob, then "Billy Bob" is your brand and people know you as Billy Bob. When the name "Billy Bob" comes up in your local community, immediately, a core set of words and associations will flash across someone's mind. "That's right, Billy Bob is a great fisherman and an amazing networker.", or "Billy Bob has a knack for classic cars". Whatever it is that you are passionate about, voice your opinions about, or just plain do very well and have shown it to others in the past is what you are known for and most likely will always be known for.

Now, that doesn't mean you can't ever change your "personal brand image". Everyday, people are constantly changing their habits, hobbies, acquiring new skills, achieving new successes and reaching new milestones. Throughout these changes, others begin to pick up the newer traits and skills that you have and eventually make it a permanent association in their memory bank. So yes, you have always and will always be in business with yourself using your own personal brand.

Right about now, you are either one of two people. The first person will say, "Oh yes, of course, I knew that all along. Thanks for sharing." The second person would remark "Wow, I never looked at it this way! This is so enlightening!". The commonality that these two people may have is that they may not proactively be promoting themselves at the level they are capable of. Thus comes in networking, the hustler mindset, and of course, the hunger and the drive to make success happen.

So, the energy has to be there. You have to be willing to step it up in life, to accept the fact and proclaim that you are sick and tired of being sick and tired, and to just take a leap of faith for once in your life (if you haven't already) and be willing to put yourself out there.

What is it going to take?

....to get to the next level?
....to do something remarkable?
....to recreate who you are as a person?
....to really make something like the event marketing industry work for you?
....to have success and do it right?

Well, I can first start off by saying that it takes a massive amount of chutzpah (or "balls", as most people would say) in order to even make that first quantum leap of faith. Most individuals who run into me, see the vision, are hungry for change, willing to do just about anything to attain the new lifestyle and have fun doing it always stuck at the same point: making the choice.

It seems so simple. To just make the choice to go all in and really embrace the more unpredictable lifestyle that is full of surprises, amazing experiences, lifelong friendships, and incredible support. Believe it or not, this is actually a worldwide dilemma. People get stuck at the point of saying "yes". They get in the rut of playing tennis in their head, going back and forth, over and over, until the cons outweigh the pros, and the person with so much potential that could have been never even set sail for the ocean. It is such a waste of amazing talent, in so many cases. Nonetheless, only YOU can make the decision to go all in and make it work for you. The only thing getting in the way of your success is YOU.

Besides having a lot of balls to lace up and run the marathon, you have to of course make the commitment as well. Without commitment, who are you kidding? Sit down, write out your goals on paper, envision your success, do whatever it takes to get to where you want to be. It all starts, however, with the full commitment. Too many great people out there these days are making audible commitments on a daily basis and never following through. They say they're going to do something, they half-arsed believe in it, and never follow through on the commitment. The main reason, in most cases, is disbelief.

Disbelief that things will not work. Disbelief feeds fear, and over time, fear takes over and all hope is lost. If there is one thing I have learned in the 7 years in the event marketing industry, when an opportunity presents itself, you have to unarm yourself of all past life events and all presumptions you may have of life itself and the way things should be done, and just say "yes". Eventually, I will cover when to say "no", but in the beginning of any game, you must be willing to say lots of "yeses" before you start getting picky and saying "no". The opposite is true whereas you absolutely have to be armed and ready to accept and hear a large number of "no's" before hearing a "yes".

Whether you are brand new to the industry, or looking to step up your game, it is crucial to know when to jump at an opportunity and when to know when something is out of your league.

Another great weapon to have if you are even going to make it is you have to protect your reputation. You see, as of this moment, your name has become pure gold. You have found the long-lost treasure that you have always been searching for. "X" marks the spot and your name was in that treasure box.

Look no further.

Your single, most valuable asset in life will always be your name. Protect it like there is no tomorrow. Do everything in your power to maintain a clean image in your name. Already tarnished it quite a bit? Get to work on polishing it up until it is nice and shiny and everyone says great things when they hear your name thrown into the mix of a conversation. What you have on your birth certificate isn't just an ingenious mix of some letters of the alphabet.

You are looking at an opportunity. A chance to put your name on the map. A chance to make a difference. To create something bigger than yourself and be part of something enormous that is only getting bigger day-by-day. This is your moment to shine.

A drive to succeed is super critical in the event marketing arena. There are a lot of hungry people out there, and the competition will heat up. When one looks closer though, just as the lion is awake at night for predators and "works harder when the enemy is asleep", you must also be willing to work extra hard in the beginning and really make a name for yourself.

There are specific tasks and projects that must be done which we will get more into in the next eBook, and of course, I am sure you can think of some of the top of your head right now that would entail getting your name in front of the right people. Now, the most common misconception is that the harder you work, the more successful you are.

That can be true in some cases, but in most, it would mean you sacrificing every hour of your day towards work. Everyone has different values, but I'm sure most would agree that at least *some* time for family, friends and/or hobbies is also important. For that reason, it's not just about working hard, but working smart. With this e-book, my intention was to really drive home the point that although working hard is crucial and a well-respect work ethic, we must always remember not to lose ourselves in the process. I want to be able to help guide you in the right direction and do things professionally. Do them fast, but do it right as well. Clearly, I believe that most would agree with the "working smart, not hard" philosophy. Since this is a fun industry to work in and there are lots of perks, being smart about *how* you do your business becomes much more important than just the act of working alone.

Finally, one of the traits that myself or others in the industry can never teach someone, but only encourage, is the utmost drive and hunger to succeed. I have been there in the past where I tried pushing the industry to someone and literally tried to sell him or her on why they should be in the game. All of that time could have been used more wisely. You see, you're either made for it or you're not. There's always room for growth and always opportunities to expand yourself as a person. So, yes, you may come in a bit rough and doubt yourself at times, but at the end of the day, only you can sell yourself on whether or not the event industry is for you.

That is a small composition of what it takes to make it in event marketing. More in-depth and practical details will be available in my next book.

Can You Do It?

Now that you have learned about what it takes to get into events & promotional marketing, you are most likely wondering to yourself the big question.

"Can I even do this? Is this for me? Am I even capable of what could be demanded of me?"

My answer has been and always will be the same: "You'll never know until you try it."

To give you some piece of mind, here is a quick checklist of questions to ask yourself before making that decision:
1.) Do I deserve more in life?
2.) Do I feel like I'm being challenged enough at work?
3.) Do I dream of traveling the world and just living life more?
4.) Am I sick and tired of the same old daily routines?
5.) Is my bank account balance lower than I would like it to be?
6.) Is there anything holding me back at home or in my hometown?
7.) What do I have to lose?
8.) What do I have to gain?
9.) Do I like living an intense lifestyle?
10.) Do I thrive off the unpredictable?

Just like new food or new excursions, you just have to make the conscious choice to go for it and hell or high water, you must go through with it. No exceptions. The simple action of making that conscious decision in your mind and saying "yes" to yourself is the single biggest favor you can ever do for yourself. So imagine for a second that you were given 5 seconds to make the biggest decision of your life. Would your legs start trembling? Would you pass out on the spot? Or, would you look in the mirror and tell yourself that it's time for change? It's time to create new boundaries and new stories in your life. Do it for your family and friends. Most importantly, show yourself what you are capable of.

There are many times in a lifetime where we are faced with unbelievable opportunities. Quite quickly, our mind plays a quick movie of what the wonderful lifestyle these opportunities would be like, the people we would meet, what we would look like, hopefully with a big smile on our face, time slowing down, with seemingly no worries in life. It seems *so* perfect. As if nothing could go wrong. Then we immediately deflect towards the worst that could happen. We start to think of the negative possibilities, the bad events that could pass us by as a result. Then, our dreams are crushed. Instead of immediately taking action and pursuing our dreams, we base the decision to not do so strictly off of everything that could go wrong as a result of it.

What happened? We drop everything for a mere feeling of "What if everything went wrong?"

I am always constantly running into folks who have incredible potential to do event marketing and to succeed. The ability to see talent in others and to foresee high expectations has always been a talent of mine. However, even some of those folks usually let fear of refection or failure take it all away from them.

My belief is that anyone can do anything that they put their mind towards. Anything at all. To start and to do it is the easy part. To endure and persist is the true test of the human character.

What does it take to endure in promotional marketing? It truly takes grit, persistence, and commitment to do whatever it takes. To not let the little things get to you and ruin everything you worked so hard for. To truly be in for the long haul.

Now, look at your current day-to-day life and how you are living? Do you *truly* feel you are giving everything you have to the world? Are you contributing enough value to the marketplace, and globally?

Think about the last time you accomplished something. When you did something great. When you overcame all obstacles and came out up top. Did it feel good? Did you feel on top of the world? Like nothing else mattered?

Most likely, you were so wrapped up in the moment, you didn't stop to think about the struggles you took to get there. The moments where you felt that you would lose it all. Where perhaps, you yourself felt that all hope was lost and the fight was not worth the struggle, the pain, and the anger.

Now think about that for a second. When something good happens to you in your life, most times, you are in the moment right? You forget everything it took you too to get there. And sometimes, you might remember *exactly* what it took and what you went through. Ask yourself this now: Was it worth the fight? All of your victories, all of the accomplishments, the big wins?

If the answer is yes, then you know that anything worth accomplishing is worth the chase. The early mornings. The late nights. The ridiculous amount of workload from time to time. The risks. The unforeseen circumstances. Those instances where we feel we are diving off a cliff to our doom, but everything turns out ok.

Time To Grab Your Bootstraps

When was the last time that you worked hard? I mean, worked really, *really* hard? I'm talking about those times where you wished you were either doing something else instead, not because of preference, but rather because of the large workload. You might have even gone so far to hate your life for it. But then, at the end of it all, was it truly worth it? Was it worth the struggle? I'm willing to bet that your answer is yes.

These are the times where we never forget the grueling hours, the incredible mental endurance, and even more, the tired commutes home. We are tested beyond our usual extremes. Pushed beyond our boundaries and, at first, causing us to second-guess the initial decision to even begin.

You and I both know that it is when you buckle down and go all-in, that you see the biggest results in life. Yes, there will be failures and you will have many challenges. That's what makes it all fun and games, plus the rewards that come at the end of it all.

Finding yourself sitting at home, wondering what is next? Are you just waiting for *something* to happen, praying that God will answer your prayers?

Stop waiting and do something. In the world of promotional marketing, nothing happens for those who just *wait*. I like to describe the work that we receive (when just simply waiting by the phone and maybe even watching some television), the "bottom-of-the-barrel" work. The work that no one else is willing to snatch up. The work that just "comes to you". I am by no means saying that it is never good to take this work, but where is the challenge in that?

Don't you want a challenge? Don't you want to reap what you sow? In event marketing, you truly get out of it what you put into it. For those road warriors and brand ambassadors who have been doing this for awhile, there's a common thread among all of them: hunger. The desire to succeed, a drive beyond what we normally see.

PART III
EXERCISES
&
NOTES

EXERCISE A

We've all been there. You learn about the wonderful world of promotional marketing, perhaps you do a gig or two, and then the big question hits: Is this something that I can ACTUALLY do?

Then, you start to have all the good things about promos go through your mind, but more likely, the bad.

You get down in the dumps, trying your hardest to believe that everything will be alright and that you can do it, but fighting the negative (or the cons) of promotional marketing.

In my experience, I have found that the pros ALWAYS outweigh the CONS in this industry.

For that reason, after working with numerous clients over the years, I was inspired to write this piece to hopefully lessen the beginning hump of getting started and making sure that this industry is right for you:

Question #1: Am I risk-averse? Do I like to take chances from time to time?

Question #2: Do I like adventure?

Question #3: Can I answer simple emails and constantly make sure that my "gig-funnel" is full?

Question #4: If I were to have to wait for a check for 4 weeks, could I survive?

Question #5: Am I willing to be flexible and make sacrifices on a day-to-day or week-to-week basis?

Question #6: Am I willing to work crazy hours sometimes, or drive across the country last minute in order to attend awesome events and get amazing pay?

Question #7: Am I willing to drop everything from time to time to work an awesome event and get cool with a new company?

Question #8: Am I willing to go above and beyond for a company to get on their good side? Even if it means doing big things that may seem impossible at first glance?

Question #9: Am I willing to stand on my feet for up to 12 hours or more a day (in the heat or cold)?

Question #10: Am I willing to be accountable to my own success and communicate, communicate, communicate?

EXERCISE B

How Much Time Do You Have To Devote To Promotions?
This is a quick exercise to do if you are not sure if you can do promotions part-time, full-time, or at all!

This is a two-part exercise, so make sure to take 10-15 minutes to do this and complete it. If not done completely, you won't get much out of it. So make sure to set aside the time!

Supplies Needed:

√Pen/Pencil
√Piece of paper/Notepad
√Quiet area where you can focus

Exercise #1

First and foremost, turn off all distractions (yes, including your phone and computer!), and clear your mind. If you need to play some meditative music, do that. Or perhaps you have a place you like to call your sanctuary, so go ahead and head there.

Let all of your worries and frustrations go.

Now, take a deep breath and close your eyes.

Imagine your perfect day.

What would it look like?

How would you start your day as soon as you woke up?

What would you do first?

Would you sleep in? Go workout? Take a walk in the park?

How about afterwards? Lunch? Go volunteer?

Or would you be working, doing something you love?

Be as detailed as possible!

Take a good 5-10 minutes, and write out as much as possible, with as much vivid detail as possible (use all five senses, what it would look like, taste like, feel like, smell like, so on and so forth). If done correctly, you will end with a huge smile on your face and several pages written in complete detail. This should give you something to look forward to and an amazing vision to strive for. Your new vision of your ideal day will play a huge role into your big "WHY". Why you are doing this, why you are working so hard, and what your purpose is.

Exercise #2

There are 168 hours in a 7-day week.

How do you know how much time you have to give towards this industry?

Let's find out!

This is a fun exercise and should take you no more than 5 minutes to complete.

Calculate the following in hours total for the week:

√**Work/Job:** _____
√**Commute Time:** _____
√**Exercise:** _____
√**Meals:** _____
√**Social Life:** _____
√**Family Time:** _____
√**Sleep Time:** _____
√**Other Activities:** _____

Add all of these activities, take the total hours, and subtract it from 168.

This is your magic number. This is how much time you have to devote towards promotional marketing.

If you result was 15-20 hours, you should consider going part-time (at least to start).

If your result was 30-40+, you should consider going full-time!

Hopefully this will help give you some clarity and comfort in knowing that you are moving forward with realistic expectations!

EXERCISE C
(CONTRIBUTED BY KRYSTIE PHANNARETH)

<u>Professional Resumes</u> are an outline of your education, skills, certificates, jobs and objectives you have for your career. It's hard to put your Brand Ambassador/ Promotional Model/ Model experience because most of the events are very temporary and would fill a professional resume with too many misc. positions that may make you look like you are a job hopper.

<u>Talent Resumes</u> are an outline of photo shoots, events and promotions you have done. These are usually 1-5 day events and don't usually last much longer, i.e. Temporary Positions. I only outlined my professional resumes skills in a talent resume if they are directly related to photo shoots, events and promotions. Such as a marketing degree, working as an event manager for a promotional company, a one-time photography gig. Update this resume after everything you do that applies to your talent. Also post any skills that may be inappropriate for your professional resume but apply to your talent, such as: golf, gymnastics, being physically flexible, race care driving, polo, and horseback riding. Let's face it, putting the fact that you're flexible on your professional resumes should mean your schedule not your body!

What you should have in your talent resumes:
Name
Email
Phone Number
Stats (such as: Height, Weight, Hair Color, Bust Size, Dress Size, Waist, Hips etc.)
Talents
Experience
Links to any videos you may have done (note if it's adult in nature)
Social Media Links if they are applicable
If you're willing to travel
Any other pertinent information
A Professional Head shot
Include any Training, Lessons or Classes you have regarding your talent

What you should leave out of your talent resume:
You're life story
Anything negative

Your relationship status
Anything to do with your children (if applicable)
Vague experience (you should be as detailed as possible without rambling)
Lies about yourself, who you've worked with and what you did
Using profanity
Unprofessional wording or sentences
Incorrect Grammar
Misspelling of words
Incomplete areas of your resume
An Unprofessional head shot (not something well taken with a cell phone)
A disconnected phone number
An email address you check only occasionally
Social media links that are unprofessional
Social media link to private profiles
Social media links that show unprofessional posts or have unrelated posts or pictures
Overly complicated design

As an example, here is my promotional marketing resume:

EXERCISE D

Brand Ambassador Action Plan

1.) Having a Vision and Creating Goals
   -What do you want out of life?
   -How hard are you willing to work for it?
   -What is it that you want to accomplish with events specifically?

2.) Setting Goals That Are Right For You
   -Not every event is for you
   -Try not to "take everything that comes your way". It's ok to be selective.
   -Write out 10 goals of what you want to achieve in the next 90 days financially, career-wise, and personal development-wise.

3.) Lining Up Type of Events with Your Skill Assets
   -There are two approaches to applying for events: investigate or rapid-fire
   -The problem with rapid-fire is that it is like a lottery system, you lose more than you win.
   -Most people use the rapid-fire approach because of their lack of understanding

4.) **Getting Things in Place**
   -Create a professional email template (samples can be found online)
   -Get a quick logo created with your name at Fiverr.com
   -Make sure to use the same email signature in all of your emails
   -Create a professional email (usually just your name @gmail is perfect)
   -Revisit your social media profiles and photos (LinkedIn is PRIORITY!)

5.) **Ramping Up**
   -Now that everything is in place, you can get started.
   -Create an email body template that you can use when applying to jobs (tweak and customize for each situation, either way, this will save you a lot of time)

-Check your emails at least 2-3x daily and get back to postings right away. DO NOT PUT IT OFF!
-Start applying for gigs and watch the replies come flowing in!!!

Thank you so much for reading "The Brand Ambassador Handbook" and I hope that you got great value from it.

Want to share your thoughts on the book with the author? Simply send an email to Edwin@promorockstar.com and I will make sure to get back to you as soon as I can. I care about your opinion and how I can improve my future works moving forward.

Want to know what agencies can help you land your next gig? Please visit http://bit.ly/PRMasterAgency and we will be constantly updating with new companies, website, etc.

Make sure to check out our Facebook group of over 10,000 brand ambassadors at http://www.promorockstar.com/group.

For coaching opportunities, please send an email to info@promorockstar.com

For further training, please visit http://www.promorockstar.com/courses

Thank you
And good luck on
your journey
to greatness as a brand ambassador
in life, your career, or even
your own business.

NOTES

NOTES

www.ingramcontent.com/pod-product-compliance
Lightning Source LLC
Chambersburg PA
CBHW071820170526
45167CB00003B/1390